Foundation of Fire:
How to Step Into Your Personal Power & Manifest Your Dreams

Lori

to the discovery of who you are

♥ Smalls

xoxo

www.foundationoffire.com

Limits of Liability and Disclaimer of Warranty
The author and publisher shall not be liable for your misuse of this material. This book is strictly for informational and educational purposes.

Warning - Disclaimer
The purpose of this book is to educate and entertain. The author and/or publisher do not guarantee that anyone following these techniques, suggestions, tips, ideas, or strategies will become successful. The author and/or publisher shall have neither liability nor responsibility to anyone with respect to any loss or damage caused, or alleged to be caused, directly or indirectly by the information contained in this book.

Publisher
10-10-10 Publishing
Markham, ON
Canada

Printed in the United States of America
ISBN: 978-1-77277-144-2

Dedication

I dedicate this book to you.
May you open your heart to the true meaning of your power, moment by moment, layer by layer and keep making the choice to step in and live your dream.

About The Author

Jessica Smalls is the creator of Budding Hearts Academy, an organization that specializes in spiritual development. Combining her own natural and psychic abilities with energy healing, along with a great sense of humor, pioneering spirit, diverse and challenging life experiences, Jessica walks with people shining her light to light the way until they can do so themselves. A visionary and teacher, creating personal and spiritual development courses, her own music and writing books, including her first, *Lifestyle Change Made Easy: Your Step by Step Guide to Change* in 2010, Jessica lives in Petrolia, Ontario, with her husband, Denver, daughters, Ruby and Hazel, son, Corbin and their two crazy dogs, Shiloh and Lady.

Foreword

I am excited to introduce you to Jessica Smalls' book, *Foundation of Fire*. Her dedication to speaking her truth and standing in her power is truly inspiring! Jessica's message of spreading love is a vital and necessary truth in today's world. She will teach you that the best way to spread love is by loving yourself first. You need to discover the meaning in your image, your words, and the vast spiritual world waiting for your silence and stillness.

Her simple how-to is highly achievable. While she reveals to you that simple doesn't always mean easy, her personal journey and process reminds you to take life one step at a time. Developing your connection to your personal power is best done at "turtle-speed" for lasting results. YOU create your own destiny!

Devote yourself to the practices and rituals outlined in this book. Your perspective about who you are will effortlessly shift as you create the life of your dreams. Read the pages within this book to practice and apply Jessica's teachings with purpose because you are worth it.

Raymond Aaron
New York Times Bestselling Author

Acknowledgments

This book is dedicated first to me. Everything I do is first for me, then for others. I have struggled, I have powerfully forged forward and I have spent many years pretending on the outside while I was secretly clawing my way out of the darkness within me. I have survived. I spent many years running from who I was. I spent many years more, comfortable living in the chaos of life, believing that I was unworthy of experiencing the peace and power that I always felt within me. This book is an act of stepping into my own personal power and the manifestation of my own dreams. I thank me.

None of this would have been possible without the entourage of support people in my life.

To Denver: You were and remain my constant supporter, the light in my darkness that first illuminated my path. You have been through the thickest, toughest, messiest moments with me. I am honored to walk by your side. The expression of who I am would not have been possible without your unconditional love for me, or without your strength and example of who you are. I thank you.

To my children: Ruby, Hazel and Corbin, each one of you are incredible teachers. Each one of you woke me up in a way that opened me to how powerful I am and how I could survive as Woman and Mother. Each of you has a profound effect on my life and I will always strive to live in line with the teachings you bring into it.

I thank you for the lessons to date and the lessons to come. I may not look like I appreciate the ultimate reflection you are for me. One day you will understand, and until that day I remain your humble Mama, forever loving you all to bits, while devoting as much of myself as I can to support each of you in your very individual journeys. I would not be who I am today without birthing each of you into this physical world. I thank you.

To my Shamans, Dusk and Two Claws: I am forever your student. I thank you for always loving me and accepting me back into the fold each time I returned from running from who I was. It is your patience and guidance that has allowed me to believe in myself, to learn what balance is and to recognize who I am. I look forward to many more lessons.

To all my Guides on the Other Side: For being there during my toughest lessons, never backing down, knowing and allowing me to figure it all out on my own and for sorry and not sorry. I thank me and thank you.

To all the parents I have ever had…Jeff and Judy, Mike and Stef, Al and Annette, and so many others: Thank you for your continued support of my dreams, for the lessons of strength, survival and connection.

To those I have sat in Circle with: We created the safest places to share our truth together. Thank you for always listening. Thank you for your truth as well...it allowed me, and continues to allow me, to deepen my own.

To all those who have placed their trust in me: I am bound by my promise to do no harm and remain humble. Without all of you, I cannot be. Thank you for the opportunities, past and present, to step into my power and manifest my wildest dreams.

To Raymond Aaron: You held my hand and walked with me when I needed it most. You shine your light and speak to my soul. Being in your presence and attending your events shifted a significant part of me. Thank you for believing in me. Thank you for doing what you have done with your life. Thank you for showing me that I can do it too.

To Cara: Thank you for your gentility, diligence and patience in supporting me through this process. Thank you for your words of encouragement and understanding that I felt shining through every message.

Table of Contents

Introduction

There are a variety of services offered at Budding Hearts Academy and bonuses especially for you that will be referred to throughout this book. To keep the content of each lesson presentation flowing, references ([1,2,3,etc]) will be made to services and bonuses offered throughout your reading experience. You will be able to find details about one at the bottom of that particular page.

In this book you will find a place to begin or add value to your journey. Clarity comes from the practices within that allow you to recognize and speak your unique truth, open your heart, step into your personal power, and connect to your unique giftedness.

I work with the energy of the natural elements of Fire, Water, Earth and Wind, my Ancestors in spirit and my Guides who always have my best interests at heart. My connection to our Sacred Mother Earth is strong. I am always on the lookout for animals that cross my path, plants that pop up in unexpected places, the way the wind blows, sun shines and water feels. It all holds meaning for me and it does for you too if you can find your way to slow down and listen.

There are gentle reminders everywhere about what is coming, where you need to be, and what you need to do. In this way, you are the source of your own wisdom. All you have ever been required to do is pay attention to the signs that speak to you. When you do not pay attention or second guess your signs, they become louder and more urgent. When the Earth, your body, your mind, or your children speak directly to you, it is your responsibility to stop and listen. While there may not always be a "deeper meaning" attached to your experiences, there is always a broader lesson to observe.

A Story from a Friend

"If you wake and prepare for your day to find a tree across your path, this could mean many things. Sometimes the tree can be a warning and maybe you will need to restructure your day or change your plans completely. Sometimes the tree will mean you need to clear your path. That something is metaphorically getting in your way. Sometimes it is simply a tree that fell down. Whatever the case, it is always helpful to stop and listen." (Heissler, 2016)

In these situations it can also be helpful to connect with a Guide[2] to help you navigate through your experience. This connection can prove to be invaluable and necessary for deeper understanding, personal and spiritual growth and reflects your willingness to take responsibility for your life and ask for help when you require it.

When you find you have begun to wander, feel uncertain, or feel scared and want to run away from your lessons, it is time to get vulnerable and brave and check in with your Guide. They often point out exactly what you need to be aware of so you can move forward at your own pace and in your own time. This is a sacred commitment. It will always be a journey taken side by side together until you decide to strike off on your own again.

In this fashion, the fact that you are reading this book means that you are, in a way, walking with me. I may not be holding your hand; however, I do feel responsible for your care and I have left markings along your path just for you.

Please accept the following guidance before you begin:

Notice at what point you are at in this book when you put it down, even if you are interrupted by the outside world. Notice the topic being discussed, when you shut down or get angry or irritated with the content. Notice what rises up within you. Ask yourself why it is triggering that particular response for you. Notice if there is a pattern in your life where you get "triggered". Like the tree in your path illustrates, sometimes our "gentle reminders" are simple, and sometimes they reflect deep lessons that need to be addressed so we can open our hearts to embrace the next lesson more fully.

Notice as much as you can and you will be surprised at what you discover.

Ignoring these "gentle reminders" will only get you more of the same. What we resist persists. Your part in the evolution of how you learn and apply what you have learned determines how much effort it will take to clear your path of the proverbial trees that have fallen or grown up in your way.

The lessons contained within are universal, functional and the foundation for continuation of learning. Your discovery will most likely occur in layers, so it is highly recommend you read through this material again and again. You will uncover more depth as you step inward and release the learning that no longer serves you. You will discover your own truth.

Throughout this book, you will learn about the Foundation of Fire, which are lessons passed down from ancestors in the spirit realm or "other side". The chapters follow a pattern that outlines the practices to integrate these new concepts into your life and they spell out F.I.R.E: Fundamentals, Intuition, Rituals, and Expression.

The Fundamentals are understandings that prepare you to fully embrace the Foundation of Fire. The fundamentals are slowing down, balance, putting you first, and grounding. Understanding these concepts will set the stage for you to begin to find the peacefulness you are looking for.

Intuition involves a meditative practice called TEM™, which is a practice shared by the Spirit Council of the Thirteen Grandmothers so you can connect to your inner guide for big and powerful lessons from the heart. Meditating and connecting to your heart regularly will develop and strengthen your intuition.

If you prefer guided meditation to get you started, the Budding Hearts Academy Member's Area has you covered.[1]

Rituals include four power houses for lasting change. The first is the Mirror Ritual, which will allow you to begin loving or deepen your love for YOU. The second is written and referred to as the Power of Words. Here you will uncover your unique truth to speak in a clear and powerful way.

The third is your Personal Mantra. A guide has been included for you to create your own and help is only an email away.[2] Personal mantras are the verbal practice of self-love, and go hand in hand with Mirror Ritual. The personal mantra harnesses the power of words to sway your subconscious mind to more positive perceptions.

---

[1]BONUS for purchasing this book can be found at www.foundationoffire.com. Simply select "DOWNLOAD MY BONUSES" Here you will find your FREE Guided Meditation. Jessica also offers individual guided meditations, developed just for you. Personal Guided Meditations are also part of your first hour coaching call.

[2]As part of the BONUS for buying, Jessica has made herself available for a small fee to provide support to enable you to develop the most powerful and clear personal mantra. Simply email buddingheartsacademy@gmail.com and follow the next steps provided.

The last of the four rituals is The Postulate. It is about manifesting your dreams. This is a powerful way to bypass the physical world and develop trust in the collective power of the universe.[3] Besides, time and space are a figment of your physical mind and the universe works in mysterious ways. Mysteries are what keeps life exciting.

The final block in the Foundation of Fire is Expression. Here, you will become clear about how you express yourself and what motivates you.[4]

The Foundation of Fire provides a solid foundation for transformation. Just as we have four elements in physical life (fire, water, earth, air); Fundamentals, Intuition, Rituals and Expression are the cornerstones of the foundation that will allow you to step into your personal power and manifest your dreams.

My blessings to you on your unique journey,
Jessica Little Flower Smalls

---

[3]Having performed postulates on my own and in group settings, I have developed a way for you to sit with yourself and complete it on your own with a FREE download at the Budding Hearts Academy website. To claim your FREE step by step, please visit www.foundationoffire.com and select "Download my Bonuses".

[4]Guidance in the area of your personal expression is available through coaching calls with Jessica Smalls. She specializes in helping others recognize and amplify their giftedness. If you are serious about discovering or amplifying your unique gifts, Total Transformation, Jessica's 8 week spiritual development course will provide the powerful dive into yourself you need, which includes one on one Healing sessions with Jessica. You can find course dates at www.buddingheartsacademy.com/spiritualdevelopment.

The First Journey

I found myself walking through an old wood. It was sparse and quiet and I could hear Water running.
I came upon a River wide enough to swim across. Without hesitation I stepped into its flowing depths.
When I touched the Water I understood that I was a part of it. I heard, "Life is fleeting." I felt the pull of the River in the direction of my dreams. I took a deep breath and closed my eyes. When I let out my breath I was different. When I opened my eyes I saw I was beneath the surface, swimming with the current; playing in the moment of the River. I saw fish swimming and branches stuck between rocks and mud. I could feel the Water moving around me. I was spinning and somersaulting through the essence of my Self, dashing downstream and poking my head up to break the surface of the River. Splashing and playing, the sunlight glimmered upon the ripples of the waves I was creating. I realized I was Otter.

The moment I realized I had shape shifted, I began swimming swiftly to shore. I was changing again. I stepped out of the water smelling the earthy musk of land and mud and evergreens. There was a winding trail up into the dark green forest dappled with sunlight that smelled of many other travelers, so I followed it. I made my way through the underbrush quick as Fox...because that is who I was.

My climb became steeper until I came upon an outcropping of rocks. I climbed nimbly over them to a big flat shelf at the top and poked my nose up over the edge. I could smell something that reminded me of home. I put my hands on the ledge and pulled my naked human body up to stand.

Before me there was an Old Man with long flowing white hair and a shape shifting face. Grandfather is said to have the faces of his totem animals and shift effortlessly between them. As his daughter, I am a shifter too. I enjoy full-body shifts of senses and perceptions as I learn the ways and medicines of my totem animals: Salmon, Fox, Otter, Heron, Deer, Wolf and Red Tailed Hawk. As Grandfather stepped aside, I heard his voice like a whisper of wind, "Welcome my Daughter, you are here. Welcome. Come and sit Fyre, and share my fire with me." I sat at the fire and he took a beautiful Bear skin and placed it around me. It fit perfectly, folding me into the embrace of Bear, my Mother. I have always felt peaceful with Bear energy.

Grandfather radiates humility and wisdom. His quiet strength and absolute presence are two qualities I emulate in my journey. I breathe deeply the essence of my Self: Warmth, light, and embers. Fire is calming for me. The calmer I am, the deeper I sink into meditation and the easier I can channel the wisdom of the energies that chose me at birth.

Who am I? I am Woman, steadfast in strength and courage. I am a Healer with my hands and voice and mind and possess the gifts of vision, dream-seeing, channeling and spirit travel. I am a beacon of pure golden light, warmth, support and example for the Fyre Tribe of Women, my Sisters, to come together in love, honesty and acceptance. I am a channel for the wisdom and connection of the Spirit Council of the Thirteen Grandmothers. I am Eniska, the Grandmother of the Womb.

I am always growing, learning, happening and becoming. I can live in a moment with a totem animal, share my healing gifts, be the physical Woman and Mother I am and more. Most importantly, I have recognized that I am more than enough.

The teachings within this book are my last teachings as this Spirit within a physical body. These are my last days on this plane of existence. These are the last days of contact with this Energy that once was dark and sheltered and now shines from within me. When I am gone, my body shall return to our Mother Earth and my Soul will return to the Red Star, my true home. I have been reborn since the first ones walked the Plains in small tribes. I have experienced and learned many important lessons through these ages. I am aware of them.

I am here to share the wisdom meant for the people who are willing to inherit the guardianship of our sacred Mother Earth: The keepers of the land and the re-tellers of wisdom.

I am here to speak this truth and share this wisdom with others. I am here to support others in their journey back to their understanding of wholeness with teachings that heal, inspire and lead to discovery. I am here to learn from my Sisters so I can grow. I am here to guide my children so they can change the world. I am here to share the Foundation of Fire.

"You were chosen many winters ago. You can find how you fit, walk your path like Turtle and share your teachings with the People to come. If you choose to, you and your Sisters and Brothers will inherit the Mother and will keep the Guardianship alive for the Granddaughters and Grandsons, the next generations of Healers, the Children of Light who will once again receive spiritual support from the very beginning."
~ Eniska

I have always felt connected to the ways of the First Peoples. While studying in elementary school I recognized there was something missing from my education. Even without that concept being presented to me, I felt it. Over the years I recognized that my biological heritage had Indigenous roots. My Grandmothers many generations before me were Cree and displaced by both tribal and settler conflict. My Grandfathers many generations before me were trappers and guides for the first French people arriving to North America. They married these Women.

I always felt connected with the Earth. I spent much time alone as a child and refused the influences of others, always doing what felt best for me.

At times this took me in directions that were unsafe and I felt lost. Spirit had a path for me to follow. This path has allowed me to understand. There isn't a single experience from my past that didn't contribute to getting me to where I am today or help me learn what I needed to support others the way I do. I am grateful for this understanding and for my path.

The following are a few key points to keep in mind as you dive into this material:

Like me, you are human. Like me, you will make mistakes. And like me, you will learn.

Choosing to walk your path utilizing the wisdom shared in this book will not be easy. The practices are simple, however you may find simple things to be some of the hardest things you will ever do.

I coach people, lead retreats that transform lives, create programs to help people transform by studying at home and in small groups with guidance. Yet, I am responsible for my growth only. YOU are responsible for your own transformation. You are the only one that can step into your own study of self and be disciplined. You are the only one that can choose to change.

Now, we will begin with the Foundation of Fire, then a familiar story.

Fundamentals

The Foundation of Fire first begins with the fundamentals. The fundamentals that we follow are the importance of **slowing down**, **balance**, **grounding** and **putting yourself first**.

These fundamentals are life-long practices. Beware of the Ego that may attempt to convince you that you know this already or you have got these fundamentals mastered. The learning curve of life comes as a spiral. Those who walk this path will relearn these fundamentals over and over again, always on a deeper level than previously encountered.

When you find your mind telling you that you have already done these things, it may be helpful to repeat the following:

There is always more to learn.

Chapter One: Slowing Down

"The one who travels their true pace wins their own race."
~ Jessica Smalls

The Turtle & the Hare

Have you ever heard the story of the Turtle and the Hare?

One day a hare was boasting about how fast she could run. She was laughing at the turtle for being so slow. Much to the hare's surprise, the turtle challenged her to a race. The hare thought this was a good joke and accepted the challenge. The fox was to be the umpire of the race. As the race began, the hare raced way ahead of the turtle, just like everyone thought.

The hare got to the halfway point and could not see the turtle anywhere. She was hot and tired and decided to stop and take a short nap. Even if the turtle passed her, she would be able to race to the finish line ahead of her. During this time the turtle kept walking step by step by step. She never quit no matter how hot or tired she got. She just kept going.

Now, the hare slept longer than she thought and when she woke up, she could not see the turtle anywhere! She went at full-speed to the finish line but found the turtle there waiting for her.

The moral for the purpose of this book is a little different than never underestimate your opponent. The moral of this story is for you to recognize that when you walk like Turtle, you get where you want to go, often faster than you ever thought you could. Life is not a race against anyone but yourself. Choose: run like Hare and burn out and require a break; or, walk like Turtle at just the pace you need to get where you want to go.

Slowing Down

Do you feel like you are doing too much and moving too fast? When someone asks how things are going, is your typical answer, *I am so busy*?

Where does the busyness come from?

Like the hare in the story, are you moving too fast, thinking about too many things and burning out in an attempt to get everything done? Busy has become a dangerous way to live. As a result, the beauty around you gets lost in the shuffle of life. The lessons are lost, and end up repeated over again. The subtle messages that exist solely to point you in the direction of balance pass by unnoticed. By being busy, there is a belief that there is no more room in your day for anything else, even when something else is best for you, providing you with a way to be more productive in less time.

YOU decide how busy you are.

Walking like Turtle not only means you slow down. It also means that you take very deliberate steps to satisfy what YOU want to do on your path. You may not have even considered what YOU want to do. Adults today are left feeling the need to do everything for their family, which leaves people in a state of perpetual doing and never giving any thought to their own needs.

Moms will often do for their families and others, and allow this "doing-ness" to determine their sense of worthiness and acceptance which depends solely on the whims of how other people feel about what is done for them. This kind of behavior is toxic.

Remember to take it easy on yourself. You decide how you show up in your life and a slow transition is often the most efficient. There is an opportunity to decide in each moment to be the Turtle or the Hare. All you need to decide is to take the first step, just like Turtle.

Many people are strongly influenced by this toxic behavior supported by mainstream society, which seems to amplify an untruth that everyone needs to fit the mold of what is "beautiful" or "right". The truth is you are already "right" and already "beautiful" just the way you are.

A wonderful friend once shared a saying called the Sniper's Creed: *Slow is smooth and smooth is fast.*

When it comes to slowing down, this statement speaks volumes. The proof seems to be in the movement itself. Once you are well practiced at slowing down, you may find that time does something really interesting for you. It is similar to the way kids play together and then get upset when it is time to leave because they feel as though they just arrived. Time really does fly when you are having fun, and so does life. As the wise Maia Heissler says, once you have walked like turtle for a while, that turtle straps on a rocket pack and off you go!

It literally does happen this way! All of a sudden you find yourself ticking so many things off your to do list, that there is extra room in your day. This does make it very tempting to fill the space with more stuff to do. Hang in there though, there are plenty rituals and practices you can plug into to fill this extra space with stillness and provide you the opportunity to BE and balance out all the DOING. It is wise to give the extra space that "appears" in your day back to yourself as much as possible.

Chapter Two: Balance

This book offers you many pathways to find balance. Any one standalone ritual or understanding may be just what you need. Step into all of them and you will be stepping into the Foundation of Fire, which has transformed lives already. Just knowing you don't need to do it all might be all you have ever needed to hear.

"The world works best in balance."
(Marshall III, 2001)

Balance is the essence of our survival. You might believe that balance is about existing in the middle or between the extremes. Not too hot and not too cold, may be a balance between the two like turning taps for a bath. You may find that you have denied the extreme feelings that have risen up in life, afraid of feeling negative emotions like anger, sadness, and despair.

Have you ever heard of contrast bathing? First you shower in hot water, and then you shower in cold. The experience creates a feeling of vigor and refreshment, similar to the way rebooting a computer system allows it the chance to optimally function. It was this concept and the experience of contrast bathing that initiated the following thought:

If you allowed yourself to feel the extremes of emotions without judgement, would you feel refreshed and awake after they had passed?

My Experience

After nearly 10 years of continually awakening to truths, looking back at this one experience it is shocking how profoundly it shifted my idea of balance. After Ruby was born, fear of sadness took over and it was impossible to feel happy. Later, I learned I was experiencing Post-Partum Depression (PPD).

Having experienced undiagnosed depression from a young age, when PPD hit me and I became aware of how entrenched it was in my life, a new understanding of balance began emerging. My partner did not understand why I could not simply choose happiness. I found I was attempting to remain in the "safe zone" in the shower where the water wasn't too hot or too cold, so I could be comfortable. At this point in my life I had very few people that I trusted and never spoke of my inner struggles, and still wouldn't for another five years. I felt so many pressures to be the best mom, wife and person I could be, that I became unable to do any of it.

While I created Budding Hearts Academy, raised my children as a full time Mom, participated in local community events, prepared for family gatherings, and the hundred other things that I allowed to consume my time, I continued to experience this deep sadness. I didn't understand it then. Now I recognize that I was searching for a way to feel worthy by filling my life with "stuff" because my perception growing up was that successful people did lots of things.

Today I see a different perspective. I realized that by refusing to allow myself to feel and express despair and sadness, it dampened my ability to experience the beauty, wonder and delight of a new baby. Balance is no longer searching for the middle ground so I can be comfortable. This is impossible. Our human experience is one of *contrast,* which allows us the opportunity to experience happiness, sadness, anger, despair, and excitement and move through the feelings like thread weaves cloth together. It was impossible to feel anything when I was trying to mute the extremes of my emotions. It is in BEING that I find comfort now.

Feeling

Maia once shared that all emotions are meant to be felt to their depths. You are meant to be present in the moment; sit with your feelings, have tea with them, breathe with them, speak with them, and allow them to flow through you. Just like the wind brings clouds, once your feelings begin to flow, they eventually pass and the time for entertaining them is over. The sun will shine again.

Balance does not exist on the pivot point of a pin between two extremes. It exists in the flow and movement back and forth. It is necessary to sit with your emotions as long as you feel you need to. There will always be wisdom, a gold nugget of truth to be discovered in each feeling if you take the time you need. This doesn't mean you will always be aware of that wisdom in those moments, and this is okay too.

Balance is not elusive; it is feeling, being, allowing and living through the messiness, the explosiveness and the peaceful calm. Balance is being present in our existence while letting go of the expectation of where we "ought" to be, or what we "should" feel. It is letting go of judgment, criticism and worry and letting life BE…And refusing to get hung up on the judgements, criticisms and worries of those who love you too.

Balance comes naturally when you recognize that you are human and accepting who and where you are. Balance is simply noticing that you are moving through emotions and experiences on your path, and providing yourself with enough stillness to contrast the busyness.

Three Commitments

Dusk once described the way to balance as beginning with one commitment at a time. He said once you have mastered your first commitment, it is time to add a second. Once you have mastered the second, add a third. He advised caution with ever going beyond three commitments, that it is important to seriously consider the decision of adding more to your life before taking a new commitment on.

When learning to juggle you begin with one ball, then add the second, and once you are comfortable, add the third. When juggling with three balls, you have one ball in each hand, and one is in the air. People who have learned to juggle have spent a lot of time practicing this skill.

Being comfortable with keeping three commitments, you may be tempted to add a fourth. Exercise caution with adding a fourth commitment. You will need to move faster and pay more attention until the commitment has been satisfied. As in juggling, there is a ball in each hand; there are now two balls in the air, and more room for error.

Your first "ball" or commitment must be to you if balance is what you seek. When you first look after you, everything else has a way of working out. Your second and third commitment can be whatever you want them to be: Family, job, and relationship with a partner, or a volunteer position. All of these commitments are often taken for granted and shrugged off as "just things we need to handle." Your life does not need to be chaotic. Balance is possible when you slow down and become clear about what you are committed to. YOU decide how much you want to do. Be careful though, your word and sanity hang in the balance of the commitments you take on and your ability to complete them.

Leave the old belief behind that you need to move at the speed of all the chaos that surrounds you. The speed of most mainstream society today encourages people to go to school, have a family, work a job and keep kids busy in afterschool activities. None of this is necessary, unless of course you prefer to live out of balance, or you prefer to have a million and one pots on your proverbial stove at once. There is nothing wrong with scaling back to keeping three commitments. Remember, slow is smooth and smooth is fast.

The chaos around you more easily sucks you in when you are overcommitted, especially when your commitment to yourself is an afterthought. Some of the chaos will even be your own creation, and you might feel responsible for continuing to create it.

Feelings of responsibility with too many commitments generally settle into the shoulders and neck if you are not immediately aware of them. If you have been taking on the responsibilities of the world for a long time you may not even be aware of the tension that so long ago settled in. Ignoring your responsibility to YOU and overcommitting yourself, may even show up as a stress-induced condition that flares up when you take on more than is required. Some commitments will be yours, some will resonate as another person's commitment that you feel responsible for helping them keep, and sometimes they are simply not your commitments at all. How do you know which is which?

Is Responsibility Light or Heavy?

A great question to ask yourself when you feel heavy with responsibility is:

Does this commitment feel light or heavy?

Ask yourself this question when you are faced with an opportunity to take on a new commitment, and when you feel stressed out about a commitment you already have on your plate. You may need to rephrase and ask in a different way to determine how it feels to you.

If I was no longer committed to this, would I feel light or heavy?

How light or heavy you feel about your commitments is the first step to identifying whether or not they are meant to be your responsibility. Generally, if it feels heavy, it isn't something you need to keep committing to and has the ability to take too much of your energy and wear you down. When it feels light it generally creates good feelings for you and quite possibly serves to recharge you.

Whenever you feel a situation is heavy, it is important to ask yourself follow up questions. Just because something feels heavy does not mean that dropping that particular commitment will fix everything. Asking more questions is a first step to identifying where your responsibility lies in your particular situation. If you find yourself confused or uncertain, this is an ideal time to check in with someone you trust and share your concerns around the situation you are dealing with. With practice, this process becomes easier and your answers will surface effortlessly.

When you keep three commitments it is easier to determine what is working and what is not. When you have overcommitted, your feelings and ego may get in the way of your ability to see your situation clearly. Go to the friends or Guide that asks you questions or shares stories rather than telling you what to do. You may find through simple conversation that what you need is to let go.

Win Win

If you quickly took on your commitments without thinking, now would be a good time to revisit whether it is a win win for everyone involved. Because your first commitment is to yourself, it is a complete contradiction to commit to anything where both parties do not receive mutual benefit. The mutual benefit may be as simple as feeling good about having tea with an elder so they don't feel lonely. The mutual benefit could also be about contributing fairly as partners in business together. Whatever your situation is, a win win always feels good inside. When it stops feeling good it needs to be revisited.

A responsible person is always willing to have a second look at a situation. It may not always feel comfortable to discuss changes to commitments, however it is quite necessary. Odds are if you are feeling out of balance with a particular commitment you have made, so is the person you have made the commitment to. Always be honest with it comes to giving of yourself, and be careful of continual giving with no receiving.

Releasing Responsibility

Releasing responsibility for the commitments in your life, can feel conflicting at first. Once you start though, you will feel lighter. You may even find yourself wanting to revisit all your commitments and responsibilities. This is a good thing to do regularly.

Ask yourself: Is it necessary that I do this? Maybe someone else is waiting for the opportunity. When it comes to responsibilities around the home, there is literally no need for you to be keeping everything just so. Your children can take on some tasks and learn about responsibility. Your partner may begin to understand the load you have taken on if you are looking at how much you already do. It may be helpful to create a family chart in this case and list all the responsibilities every member of the family has. It creates an opportunity for the conversation to happen and for others to naturally step up to the plate.

No one will offer to assume a commitment or responsibility from you if you are complaining about all the things you do or nagging others about completing their own. You must always ASK FOR HELP.

Asking for Help

This is a lesson that sounds simple and is not easy. It requires an enormous helping of vulnerability and an admission that you aren't the only one responsible. While it is true that you have your answers within you, you are inside your situations and unless you are disciplined at stepping into the "observer mind", you may require a Guide outside of you to point out the questions you need to ask yourself sometimes. Let's face it, you are not solely responsible for knowing what to do all the time. No one is.

It can never be said enough, that no one person is responsible for doing everything for everyone. Even you are not responsible for doing everything for YOU. You ARE responsible for asking for help when you need it though.

Asking for help means you let go of the false sense of pride that comes with doing everything on your own and in your own way. The pride a child feels once they have tied their shoes on their own for the first time is true pride. Preparing and serving a holiday dinner for many guests all by yourself (or any similar situation that comes to mind), refusing help, and then complaining or boasting about how you did it all on your own; this is false pride and borders on martyrdom. Situations like this, hurt yourself and others because you become exhausted and no one has the opportunity to learn anything, except to stay out of your way.

By asking someone for help, you are offering someone an opportunity to be a part of something, feel valued, and potentially learn a new skill. You also give yourself the opportunity to take some pressure off and create space so you can enjoy yourself. Receiving is just as important as giving, and you deserve to receive help as much as another person deserves the opportunity to give it.

Get a pencil. Take a moment to reflect on all the responsibilities you have at home. List your responsibilities on the next page.

My Responsibilities

How long is your list? If you were to create a job description for your role in your family life, how would you feel about asking someone else to take on all of your responsibilities?

If you wouldn't expect anyone take on all of your responsibilities, how can you realistically expect that of yourself? How important is it that the dishes are done immediately after dinner? How important is it that the laundry gets folded exactly how you like it? How important is it that these things you have identified as YOUR tasks are done YOUR way?

Is there possibly another way that will work just as well that might even empower someone else? Could you imagine what it would feel like to NOT NEED TO DO some of these tasks? How much space in your day and in your mind would this provide for you?

Asking someone else for help could mean you will need to teach them how to do what you do. While this may seem like a daunting task at first, it is front end loaded. All the effort comes up front, and once you have put the effort in you will be free to stick to your guns and refuse to be responsible for it any longer. Helping with a task you have released responsibility for can be helpful, but taking it back over can send a message that the person who was looking after it just isn't good enough. If you already understand you struggle with perfectionist tendencies, just walk away. BEING responsible and TAKING away someone else's responsibility are two very different things.

You & Community

This is an old way to create balance and begins with establishing a giving and receiving relationship with people you trust. Your community can be thought of as having an inner circle and an outer circle, with only you in the center. Your inner circle is strictly for your personal needs, so you can share your truth and seek a different perspective. These are people you can lean on. These people will listen when you need an ear and never repeat what has been said. They agree to never attempt to fix you. You are already whole and on your journey of rediscovery. Never believe anyone who says you are broken or that you require fixing, especially YOU!

The Grandmothers recommend your inner circle have five people in it. This way there will always be someone to listen when you are in need of a shift in perspective or an outsider point of view.

Using your body like a container and never releasing what bothers you can be hazardous to your health. It is your responsibility to keep your body feeling clean and clear. Your inner circle is for dispersing the load of heaviness that speaking your unique truth often releases. It will provide you an opportunity to feel safe and accepted, seek wisdom and say what you need to say. Your inner circle will always be strong enough to handle anything that comes up for you. No one wants anyone else to feel alone.

The next ring of community is those who help you with your external responsibilities. These are people you trust that will step up in your life and help you. These are the people you would trust with your daily tasks, your home, your children, or your pets when you are not there. Some of these people could include your children and partner. Over time they may also become people you reach out to when you need support while you are ill so you can take the time you need without feeling burdened by responsibility. They may also become people that you support in return in a similar manner. The Grandmothers suggest thirteen people in this circle.

If you are feeling a state of shock, stop and take a deep breath. This is the *suggestion* from the Grandmothers. It is meant to be used as something to move toward. If you do not belong to a close knit community already, your first step will be to begin with one person. Trust is not something that develops overnight. Do your due diligence and begin building these relationships now. Just as a child learns to count, you will always begin with one. If you want a community of mutual support, you need to take the first step.

"Receive with gratitude and give with love. This is the old way. All we need to do is claim it. There is no reason why we cannot re-establish this."
(Heissler, 2017)

Utilizing these circles will mean you can release responsibility and take a break from carrying the load of life on your shoulders all the time. First you will need to be willing to let go of the responsibilities you decided to carry. Become aware of any attachment to your worth or any value you find in remaining overcommitted. Decide which is most important to you, being committed to yourself or being committed to how people see you.

When children are born, they rely on their parents for everything. As they grow, they rely less and less and take on the responsibilities of dressing themselves, choosing what to wear, brushing their teeth, feeding themselves, walking, cooking, and the list goes on. As the parent it is your decision how much responsibility you release to your child and when. You can always choose to remain responsible for them and never release anything. If you never let it go though, one day you will find yourself carrying around a 20 year old, whom you dressed, bathed and fed. Some say doing everything is just easier. Easy is not always best. Each child must grow to be a responsible adult. This is a very slow and long process of releasing responsibility from the parent to the child over years.

Every situation will be different. The next example will illustrate just how complex it can be to determine and act when you feel responsibility rise up.

How Am I Responsible?

A grand daughter was visiting her grandmother. She found her grandmother was repeating herself, shared that she didn't feel the urge to eat regularly or really understand what was good to eat. The grandmother was concerned about driving given the "spells" she was having and she was fearful about hurting herself.

The visit was wonderful and when the granddaughter left, she felt very heavy. All through the afternoon, she felt like she couldn't take a deep breath and the visit with her grandmother popped into her mind often.

Finally, the granddaughter could not sit with the heaviness any longer. She decided that this heaviness was meant to be shared. She decided it was not her responsibility to provide care for her grandmother, and though she sincerely wanted to, she remembered that she too was a mother, wife and business woman and did not have any more space in her life for more responsibility. Despite overwhelming feelings of guilt about not willingly taking responsibility for the care of her grandmother, the granddaughter decided that it was best for her to share her concerns about her grandmother with her father and uncles. She decided it was better to continue the open, trusting and fun relationship between grandmother and granddaughter, rather than jump in to make things better.

While sharing her concerns she was afraid of being wrong. Worried her uncles would think she was meddling, she thought they might tell her grandmother what she said. She worried about how her grandmother might feel, and how their relationship might change. Despite all of these feelings, the conversation went well, her father and uncles were receptive, and they took on their own responsibilities in caring for their mother without question.

The granddaughter was relieved. She was proud of herself for standing up to the guilt, worry and fear that rose up and tried to convince her to do more than she needed to. She often wondered what her uncles thought about her sharing her concerns, and realized that if she was meant to know, someone would say.

The granddaughter in this story is a strong young woman. She knew herself and her boundaries and though she was not fearless, she was remembering her own spirit when she faced the potential responsibility of caring for her grandmother. Her worries really reflected how she felt about herself. Her father and uncles played the parts of mirrors for her in this example.

Deciding the discussion had to happen was a simple thing to do, however, being there and having it was not easy at all. The granddaughter was uncomfortable and experienced many emotions.

In the end, she kept her spirit in mind, and did her part. To this day, she can still attest to feeling "clean and clear" with herself because she felt responsible in some way and quickly decided to act on her sense of responsibility in a way that felt heavy at first and light in the end for her.

Chapter Three: You First

In chapter two, you made a list of all your responsibilities. Turn back to that list and identify which ones are the A tasks (must be done by you), which are the B tasks (could be done by someone else) and if you are able to group them in other ways, do so. When you have grouped and itemized your list, step back and take a good look at it.

Where on this list are the things you do just for you? The things you do to refuel, recharge and fill yourself up. Are they at the beginning? Are they at the end? Did you forget them? Do they even exist? Did you consider yourself at all? When you first thought about all the things you needed to do in a day, were YOU left out of the equation?

YOU matter. YOU are the most important part of your equation. Nothing can continue to be done day after day if the person taking care of the responsibilities is never cared for. It is not anyone else's responsibility to take care of you the way you care for them. It is yours. This responsibility was released to you by your parents. Your responsibility is to ask for help when you need it for the care and keeping of YOU.

Your well-being comes first. What you need to do for you must be done before you begin to do for others. When you work with energy, you ground yourself before you lay hands on anyone. Doing for yourself first can take on many forms. Get creative and tell the guilt that naturally tags along at first to take a hike.

Have you ever found yourself thinking you really needed a nap, then got busy doing dishes, or tidying up and never did take the opportunity for the nap you needed? When that happens enough, you get run down, especially when you have overcommitted. When you put yourself first there is less chance of getting run down because your needs are already taken care of.

Put yourself first and everything else is put on hold momentarily. Schedule your day the night before and spend less time thinking about the next day at bedtime. Be more prepared for the morning and you will have had a more restful sleep which always leads to better balance for handling whatever comes up the following day. Change your mind about how you are willing to operate and you will change your life.

Just like the in story of the Turtle and the Hare, while the Rabbit knew she was fast, she pushed herself too hard, and knowing she was faster, slept too long and woke up too late to win. The Turtle also knew she could do it, and chose to do it one step at a time. Each step was carefully and deliberately taken to the best of her ability. The Turtle may have finished the race slowly, but she also PACED herself. She understood that nothing can really be done well in a rush.

Intention

When you shift behaviours, thought patterns and responsibilities, you create opportunities for growth.

When your intention is clear, your road appears.
~ Jessica Smalls

In the example in chapter two, the granddaughter's intention was to be "clean and clear" with who she was. She identified that it was her responsibility to report to her father and uncles what her grandmother shared, because the alternative was too much to bear. If she had said nothing, she would have felt horrible if anything had happened to her grandmother that resulted in her getting hurt or worse. By remembering her own spirit, she reminded herself that she is not responsible for being everything to everyone, but that she had a responsibility to pass along the information. By recognizing where her responsibility was, she put herself first by doing her due diligence.

"When life tends to get overly complex, too fast, too cluttered, too deadline-oriented, or too type A for you, stop and remember your own spirit." (Dyer, 2008)

Your spirit will never steer you wrong. What gets in the way of your growth is usually what is outside of you and your feelings of responsibility about it. What is said from within your own mind can get in your way as well, if you allow it to. That beautiful and approximately ten pound weight that sits atop your neck plays a critical role. Your mind is a tool, not the boss. You can use it to create new habits, patterns and behaviours, and choose to follow through and be disciplined; or you can choose to let the thoughts and emotions overcome you and allow them to sabotage your growth.

Your INTENTION must be clear about where you want to grow and how you want to BE. This means you need to have awareness about your first step only, not necessarily your ideal end result. The end result will typically shift and change over time anyways, so to keep your intention clear and powerful, make sure it is focused on your present moment, rather than some distant future possibility or plan.

This may be contrary to what you have heard in the world about creating dreams. Remember we are discussing intentions here regarding putting yourself first. If you are waiting for a specific situation to manifest itself, you are not coming first, the situation is. It will always feel better to reach for the relief that comes from accepting your NOW and loving what IS.

Best get in touch with yourself and begin to weave your web of awareness. Life is about the beauty you discover in the contrast of situations you will experience while journeying through it. To journey through life in this manner, it is vital to learn how to ground and center yourself in your experiences. Most of the rituals that will be shared later on are about grounding energies. What is grounding all about?

Chapter Four: Grounding

You are grounded!

Did you ever hear this statement in your childhood years? Although it typically reflects a promise of some sort of punishment to help discourage wrongdoing, when said in a different tone can also be a wonderful compliment. If you look deeply at the "punishment" of being grounded as a child, it was typically about staying put (being still), and learning a lesson (developing awareness). You may also have had a period of time during your "grounding" where you needed to be quiet. Although this parenting practice may have a negative connotation for a child, it is deeply rooted in self-awareness and stillness.

Self-awareness

It is critical to become aware of who you really are. You may have learned by example that being in service is what life is about. While there is some truth in this, you have already learned that to be of service to anyone else you must be in balance, which is why YOU are the first one who requires your service.

Bringing your awareness to yourself and serving yourself first might feel selfish in the beginning. However, if you resonate with it, it might begin to feel self-full, which may be an enormous relief.

Awareness is about refusing to look to others first for what you need to do and finding your answers within. Your truth, acceptance and love have and will always be found within you. They have been patiently waiting to be discovered all along.

Awareness is rooted in knowing how you feel about taking a step and recognizing your true need to initially move slowly. Taking too many steps at once can literally leave you dizzy and unaware of your surroundings. Besides, a turtle never runs, it always takes things slow and checks out all the angles before committing to the next step.

Consider what your typical pattern has been regarding commitments in your past. Looking to your past can help you understand your innate patterns of behaviour. Knowing yourself and what you "typically" do is critical to truly and honestly stepping into your new way of being.

Stillness

"You came from a quiet, peaceful place that's the very essence of creation, so when you mind is filled with noisy dialogue, you shut out the possibility of remembering your spirit." (Dyer, 2008)

When you slow down you can see clearly. When you can see clearly, the chaos around you can be identified as outside or inside of you. With all the busyness defined, stillness is possible. Putting yourself first gives you the opportunity to begin your day in balance. Stillness is about breathing and noticing. Water running through a rapid in a river will have areas that look chaotic and areas where water doesn't move at all. Stillness typically exists within chaos and also because of chaos.

You cannot control what other people are doing. Kids get noisy, people get angry, and life can fly by at rocket speed. You are in the center of it all, and YOU are the only factor you have any influence over.

Everything is energy and has a specific vibration. When you want the vibration around you to change, you must first change your own vibration and become the calm that gives permission to others to be calm as well. Stillness is the answer. You always have a choice. You can jump into the chaos that is the life swirling around you like a tornado, or you can choose to be an observer, the eye of the storm; still, calm and powerful.

"You always have the power within you to shift into a peaceful mode." (Dyer, 2008)

The Purple Bubble

The Purple Bubble is a quick and simple visualization technique that creates the opportunity for stillness so the energy of peace and calm can grow within you.

Creating your Purple Bubble requires stillness, which is why you will always begin with three activation breaths. This breathing technique is the foundation of all rituals and practices and can be practiced anytime you like. It is a simple and powerful tool that only gets stronger over time.[5]

You can find verbal instructions on how to create the Purple Bubble and how to complete an Activation Breath for free in the members' area at www.buddingheartsacademy.com. Below are step by step instructions that you can record on a voice recorder, then listen to and follow while you are learning. This is the simplest way to learn to use this tool.

The Purple Bubble Visualization

First close your eyes and take three Activation Breaths.[6] *Continue to breathe, and visualize a point of white light in the center of your body. Imagine that this point of light is a small bubble. This bubble grows with every breath you take. Breathe in energy and then exhale this energy into the bubble. Continue to breathe energy into the bubble until it surrounds your entire body. When you are comfortable with the size of your bubble, turn it purple. Open your eyes.*

---

[5] The Purple Bubble Visualization can be found in the member's area at Buddingheartsacademy.com as part of Jessica's Thank you gift and is part of your free downloads at www.foundationoffire.com. Simply click "download my bonuses".

The Purple Bubble remains in place for 12 hours, and you decide how big you want it to be. Create a calm energy around you, the building you are in, your town, your country, the Earth itself…the only limiting factor is your own mind.

"The energy of your thoughts determines whether or not you're living at an inspired level, so any doubt in your ability to manifest your desire or to receive spiritual guidance is vibrationally out of tune with that desire." (Dyer, 2008)

The Purple Bubble can be used while travelling. Vehicles have been observed as literally moving away from the vehicle in the center of the bubble. In this way it can provide safe travel wherever and however you want to travel.

This is an ideal tool to use before going to work if work is particularly stressful or challenging. Because it calms down your vibration and allows you a moment to be still, using it when putting children to bed is also highly effective. Children are natural mirrors to the energy you exude. Your calm helps influence theirs.

Calm and peaceful energy is a higher vibration. When people come into the space of a higher vibration they will either rise to that vibration to match it in harmony, or if their vibration is too low, they will leave the space of their own accord.

Notice what happens within and all around you when you create your Purple Bubble. When you do this you are grounding your own energy to the center of your being. In the next chapter, you will be grounding your energy to the Earth. Practice the Purple Bubble as much as you can, then note the differences in how it feels to ground to your center versus the center of the Earth once you begin TEM™.

Intuition

"Trust your own intuition – no one else has to agree with you or even understand you. Remember, your goal is to feel good." (Dyer, 2008)

The second building block in the Foundation of Fire is Intuition. Intuition is something you were born with., and it shows up differently for everyone. Whether it is a twinge in your gut when something doesn't feel quite right, a knowing, a voice, or a sense; it is real.

Your intuition is like a muscle that needs the opportunity to grow. For intuition to grow, you need to listen to it and heed it. When you do, you are likely to avoid circumstances you would rather not be in. When you ignore it, not only does it atrophy just a little each time, you may also find yourself in a sticky situation.

My Experience

When I was 17 years old, my parents went away for the night. I didn't prefer to drink or party, but many of my friends did. This particular weekend was a party weekend and a few kilometers away from our house there was a big party going on. Sometime that weekend, I received a phone call from a friend who was at this big party and was requesting rescue. I had access to a vehicle so I could get to work, and my parents specifically requested that they want their car at that party.

I felt badly when my friend called. I told her I would be right over to pick her up and we arranged a meeting place. When my sister and I were walking from house to garage, I had this feeling that my parents were going to pull in any moment. They weren't due back until the next day, so I ignored the feeling, and my sister and I got into the car. When I opened the garage door, my parents were coming up the driveway. I turned the car off and we both got out of the car.

This was my intuition speaking to me. I ignored it and endured the discomfort of coming face to face with being caught disregarding my parents' wishes about their vehicle.

Chapter Five: TEM™

"Along with praying or communing with your Source with peace in your heart, you must 'be still.' This means taking time to get quiet before meditating, and also monitoring your breathing." (Dyer, 2008)

Transcendental Elemental Meditation, or TEM™, combines Activation Breathing in a comfortable position and location with the energy of any number of natural elements (fire, water, wind, and earth). You allow yourself to step outside your current situation to listen to the wisdom of that particular element or combination of elements. This wisdom is then integrated into your heart for greater understanding. The purpose of TEM™ is to create an opportunity for reconnection with natural elements. These elements have wisdom to share, they have life force energy and they are powerful tools to call on when you need them.

This type of meditation requires some specific practice with breath play, called Activation Breathing. Breathing in this manner activates your innate sense of worthiness and power, allowing you to focus, be still and eventually, without realizing it, relax in meditation mode.

Establishing your practice with TEM™ is quite simple. You will receive your own meaning from your practice. You may find yourself journeying, day-dreaming, sleeping, noticing messages, or simply wading through the thoughts stuck in your mind. All results are acceptable.

Where to Meditate

You can do this form of meditation wherever you want, be in any comfortable position you want, and choose whichever natural element calls to you each time. Simply learn the breathing technique and allow yourself to go where you go. Let go of all expectations around a specific result from your TEM™ experience. Allow it to be whatever you need it to be.

TEM™ is meant to be effortless, and through effortlessness, profound meaning can emerge. Part of this process will be learning to trust your intuition. Trust your experience and take everything as it comes. Trust. Is. The. Key. Doubt will only sabotage your growing intuition. Whatever your experience ends up being, even when it is total blackness and nothingness, trust that you have been successful and received exactly what you needed.

Ultimately, TEM™ is about finding your guide inside, trusting the wisdom that comes to you and strengthening your intuition.

What to Meditate With

If you choose to meditate with water, it is best to have water nearby or be in water in some way, for example; in a bath, foot bath, floating on water, standing or sitting in or beside a stream, with a bowl of water, and even acknowledging the water in your own body.

If you choose to meditate with earth, be naked on the ground, have your feet bare on the ground, sit under a tree, hold a rock, stick or flower, or recognize the earth within you. Earth meditations are very special, because Earth has so many facets to meditate with that have their own unique life force energies.

If you choose to meditate with air, be outside, acknowledge the air moving through your body, stand in the wind or simply focus on the breath.

If you choose to meditate with fire, light a candle, create a fire in a safe and responsible place, or connect with the fire inside you.

When to Stop Meditating

When you feel that you are complete in your meditative experience is the moment you are done. Allow yourself the time to slowly come back to the world again. As your intuition grows stronger you will feel your end coming and naturally bring yourself out. Feel free to meditate for a minute or two when you can, or for hours if you have the space and time to do so. Whenever you meditate you are being still and going as slow as you are able, so the length of time you spend in meditation is not really of consequence.

Next is a Guided Meditation you can use for grounding your energies to the earth. Earth energy is very special and a truly powerful grounding technique. This can be found in the members' area online as well.[6]

Grounding to Earth Guided Meditation

Take three slow Activation Breaths and bring yourself to this moment. Embrace and appreciate your present moment. You are deeply and profoundly loved and supported in every moment regardless of your situation. Trust that all your needs are being met.

Create spaces in your home where you can feel absolutely at peace. In doing so, you create a template of peace for all areas of your life.

Feel the solidity and power of the Earth beneath you. This is in your core. Just as grass pushes up out of moist ground, know that fresh new shoots of growth are taking root within you right now. You are grounded, prosperous, and strong. As you breathe, breathe groundedness, prosperity, and strength into your being.

---

6 BONUSES for purchasing this book can be found at www.foundationoffire.com. Simply select "Download My Bonuses". Here you will find your FREE Guided Meditation. Jessica also offers individual guided meditations, developed just for you. Personal Guided Meditations are also included as part of what you receive after your first hour of Guidance.

Activate the Spirit of Earth within you by noticing how your physical body relates to, and identifies with, the physical world around you. Let the reality of your relationship with the Earth fill your consciousness. Feel it everywhere. Let yourself merge with this energy. Imagine yourself as a hillside. Breathe in this experience. Imagine yourself as a mountain. Breathe in this experience. Imagine yourself as a canyon. Breathe in this experience.

Imagine yourself laying in a meadow of wildflowers. In the distance there is a grove of trees. Choose one tree and be one with it. Feel the strength of the tree, the roots of the tree. Set your feet down into those roots and extend them down deep into the soil, reaching down, down, down to wrap around the center of the Earth. You are connected. Breathe deeply and feel this connection to Mother Earth fill your being. You are one.

Rituals

"When you make the decision to become a being of sharing, and practice keeping your thought harmonized with spirit energy on a daily basis, your purpose will not only find you, it will chase after *you wherever you go."*
(Dyer, 2008)

Rituals are sacred practices. The rituals shared in the following section were all taught by Guides on the Other Side. All of the following rituals have been and are still being practiced.

My Experience

I have practiced Mirror Ritual since 2011, Power of Words since 2010, and Personal Mantra since 2012. The Postulate is a ritual I was able to put a name to three years ago, when I recognized I had been doing it without knowing since I was a child.

Utilizing all four of these rituals in my life, I have totally transformed myself and will continue to transform as I head down my life path.

If I had to choose one ritual from this book to recommend to you, it would be Mirror Ritual. It has by had by far the greatest impact on my personal and spiritual development and continues to keep me in a state of humility and grace. Sharing the Mirror Ritual was part of my initial reason for writing this book. The Grandmothers are also in agreement it is time the information was no longer a secret.

Chapter Six: Mirror Ritual

This ritual is for those who wish to know who they truly are. It is a simple thing to do, and it is also the hardest thing you will ever do.

Speaking Your Truth Out Loud

There is a speaking piece to this ritual. Choose how you wish to begin speaking to yourself before you begin. A few ideas for beginning are:

"I am beginning to accept my….."
"I am beginning to love my ….."
"I love my….."

Remember that these words must be your truth. You must be honest with yourself. Give yourself the opportunity to "try on" which statement feels right for you. If none of these ideas match your feelings, then create your own statement.

When creating your own statement, you MUST always begin with "I am….." There is power in these words. These are now words. Your statement must also be kind.

Eye Contact & Body Language

Eye contact and body language are important elements for Mirror Ritual. Each element plays a role in the development of a powerful session.

When you begin your Mirror Ritual, you are standing naked in front of a full length mirror or a mirror that you can easily see your whole body in at once. You must connect with yourself by looking into your own eyes. Throughout the ritual, be sure to come back to your eyes. Your truth is here, and by making eye contact you are checking in with yourself. Other than these moments of eye contact, your eyes must not look anywhere other than your body. Other than blinking, your eyes must never close.

Your body language also needs to be open. Stand with feet slightly apart and your arms by your sides. Crossing your arms, holding hands behind your back or in front is hiding parts of your body from your view. It is important that you see all of you.

My Experience

Looking into my own eyes is powerful. I hold myself highly accountable to maintaining eye contact and mindfulness during my Mirror Ritual. I need to do this for myself. I am notorious for glazing over things, especially when it comes to my own development. This is one of my ways I am honest with myself about who I am. I experience frustration when I realize I have looked away from myself. To teach myself not to look away, I thank myself (this always sounds like "thank me") and start from the beginning. When I realize I am not in the moment (thinking, daydreaming, etc.) and am simply going through the "motions", I also thank myself and start from the beginning again.

Go Slow

This ritual is meant to be a sacred and tender moment. Make sure you have enough time to complete your mirror ritual. You may need to plan ahead and make more time for yourself so you don't feel rushed. Remember that the Turtle in the very first chapter learned that nothing is ever done well in a rush. Take your time and notice.

When to Do Your Mirror Ritual

Your Mirror Ritual is done as the first thing you do in the morning, unless you need to use the washroom because that might create a feeling of being rushed. It is also the last thing you do before you go to bed at night.

Where to Do Your Mirror Ritual

Choose a space to practice your Mirror Ritual that feels safe to you. You will be standing naked, so you may want to be in a room with a door that locks from the inside. Remember your ritual is sacred, and it is about your relationship with you, so bystanders are not necessary.

The Mirror Ritual

Be completely naked and stand in front of your mirror. With your hands open, begin with your hair and slowly move your hands over your hair three times while saying the statement you have decided to use.

"I am beginning to accept/love my….."

Follow the exact same process for your face, neck, breasts, arms, hands, stomach, legs, and back (turn slightly so you can see it).

For womanhood and manhood (sex organs) make a triangle with one hand over the other and place them over your woman/manhood and take three breaths before you speak.

Always end at your bum (turn slightly so you can see it). Move your hands slowly over it three times, speak your choice of words, *"I am beginning to accept my bum because it follows me everywhere."* Please giggle if you wish. It is helpful to end your ritual with a smile.

Mirror Ritual gives you an opportunity to be brave, vulnerable and honest with yourself. Acceptance and love will result from your continued practice and perseverance. Love truly can change your life when it comes from inside you.

Practice & Perseverance

Practice every morning and every night. When you forget to practice, thank yourself for remembering, and do not let yourself off the hook. Make up for your missed opportunity as soon as you can. By acknowledging your miss-step and forgiving yourself, you are committing to ending negative self-talk. Give yourself breaks from negative self-talk as much as possible. It serves no purpose but to keep you down.

Perseverance is necessary for your personal and spiritual development. It strengthens your resolve to keep going. Like a bow being pulled back, you will launch yourself forward into your next wave of self-discovery.

"If one doesn't find a way to do what is necessary, it's easier the next time to find a way not to act." If one can do the necessary and sometimes seemingly mundane things, one has within himself or herself to persevere when it becomes necessary." (Marshall III, 2001)

How have you persevered?

My Experience

I persevered by being home with my children so I could support them through their impressionable years. This was no easy task for me, as I preferred to be working outside the home. I cook all our food from scratch because I believe it is healthier and because we have a list of food allergies that we deal with.

I persevere by remembering to practice my Mirror Ritual every morning and night, whether I am staying over at a friend's place, in the woods, at a conference, or in my room. I ran away from myself, my mirror and my Guides enough times to know how it feels to unconditionally love and forgive myself. Take care of the little details and plug away and you will find the strength to face yourself and love yourself every day.

I have often found myself on adventures where I felt I had no other choice but to continue forward. I will share two of these stories with you. Each story is an experience I remember very clearly and come back to when I need to dig deep to move forward.

Many Socks

I was on my very first interior canoe trip with Denver, my boyfriend of nearly one year. We went for 8 days deep into Algonquin Park. This was all new to me and I fell in love with the simplicity. On the second morning, I realized my moon time had come. I had just ended a nine day cycle the week prior to our trip, so you can imagine my surprise. The surprise was replaced with mortification when I realized that I hadn't brought any feminine products on the trip with me. I immediately went into "survivor" mode. I made camp and unpacked my clothes. I had brought along 5 pairs of socks for this trip. Denver told me I wouldn't need them, but I was adamant and brought them along. I was so happy I followed my intuition, because my many socks saved me. I strung the clothesline and began cutting, boiling and drying my socks. I used duct tape to create pockets in my underwear to hold the socks to absorb my moon blood.

When Denver woke up to find camp made, coffee ready and me boiling socks, he was a little confused. He says to this day, that although he didn't realize it in the moment because he was kind of grossed out, seeing me take initiative and create a solution to my situation was the moment he knew that I was the woman for him.

Ride the Waves

On another interior trip I was just pregnant for my first time. It was spring and we were headed out of the Algonquin Park interior via Lake Opeongo. This lake is 14km long and known for being wild and unpredictable. On this particular day it was cold and we had white caps on the water, the wind was so strong and wild. We hugged the shore the entire way. Once we needed to cross a bay. We left shore and Denver's wedding hat (the hat he wore when we married) blew off his head. We realized it was too dangerous to try to retrieve it.

I just about lost my mind! I was crying, worried we might capsize and scared that if we did I might lose the baby I worked so hard to conceive (it was a long and very interesting process).

There was nothing Denver could say or do to calm me because I couldn't explain why I was so scared at the time. He encouraged me to just keep paddling when I was begging to land the canoe and wait out the winds. He told me it was more dangerous to land than to keep paddling, so I hunkered down and listened to him. After all, he had far more experience than I did. I paddled through my tears, wet and cold and nauseous from early pregnancy and just kept repeating loudly, "I can do this."

We went the full 14kms while my talented husband steered our course safely with skill he had honed over years of practice. He had seen worse than that day. I kept going and we did it together. He told me that one day I would look back at this experience and it would help me, and he was right. It is a lesson in perseverance, and has since been a source of my own strength that I remind myself of.

Allow your Mirror Ritual to be the opportunity you need to develop perseverance, and where you continue to persevere.

Why Mirror Ritual?

There is always something beautiful right under the surface. How often do you look at your reflection with judgmental eyes that seem to automatically identify what needs to be fixed, changed, or covered up? How many times have you looked at yourself, clothed or not, and passed judgement for your own appearance?

Your physical body is the only one you have. You might feel pressure from society to meet a specific physical standard, or that pressure could feel like it comes from inside. What you are feeling is grossly misunderstood. You see, you came into this world a being of pure love and acceptance. Your physical conditioning (what you observed, heard and were told) was contrary to what you knew in your heart.

Society wants us to believe in the consumerism of a system that thrives off your feeling inadequate so people can make money. Instead of utilizing honest practices and spreading the message of acceptance, consumer society has been spreading the message of unattainable perfection for a very long time. This message has been intricately woven into movies, advertising, print, fairy tales, and has become the thoughts that run through your mind. This system thrives on comparison to others. YOU can only thrive on self-acceptance and self-love.

This misunderstood feeling is very simply the conflicting beliefs of your heart and mind. Your mind has been influenced by what it has seen and heard over the physical years of your life. Your heart has only ever been influenced by your Spirit and your innate knowing that is as timeless as the universe itself.

Maia shared a simple analogy of why it feels so difficult to get to your destination of a body you can love:

"If you need a new fridge, and you walk into Sears and the sales person calls you ugly, and then attempts to sell you a fridge…you will not feel like buying a fridge from him." (Heissler, 2017)

Similarly,

"If you treat your children like most people treat their bodies, they will never cooperate. Every cell in your body is tuned in to your thoughts, emotions and behaviours, just like children are. Children need to feel loved and respected if you want them to cooperate with you. Treat the cells in your body like children that need to be loved. This physical body is a gift. This is why it is so essential to be a good friend to your body. Your body has been waiting its whole life for you to acknowledge its beauty and simply love it just how it is right now." (Heissler, 2017)

Mirror Ritual is accepting the way you are right now with kindness and love. Your kind words of acceptance and your gentle gaze into the mirror at your body morning and night will change how you feel.

My Experience

When I first began my Mirror Ritual, I noticed that the majority of my actions were against loving me. This meant I needed to restructure my entire life in ways that I didn't quite fully understand, simply because I didn't love myself yet. It felt overwhelming and impossible.

By the end of the first year of practicing my Mirror Ritual, I cried in front of my reflection when I heard myself saying "I love my…" rather than "I am beginning to love my…" It took a year; persevering morning and night, pushing myself because I understood the value of what loving myself could do for me. I did everything I could for everyone I loved and I wanted to show myself that kind of commitment. I began loving myself in ways I never thought were possible. Once I loved myself, what needed to happen effortlessly happened when it needed to.

Persevering with Mirror Ritual meant I needed to surrender to my own vulnerability, which often felt like it came at the expense of my pride. When I surrendered my pride, what I found was a truth deep inside me that began surfacing, because each time I stepped in front of the mirror, I stopped hiding from myself. Whenever I stopped or forgot it was because on some level I didn't want to face my truth.

My Mirror Ritual has changed over the last 6 years of practice, and it has become the most important element of my daily self-care routine. By making it a habit, I found I had something to work with when I was feeling low. Mirror Ritual is an important part of my spiritual practice too, and I credit it as something that I did to save my own life.

It helped me recognize I was worthy of being the vessel of divine light that I am. I stopped running away from who I was and I began to step into my power and be who I am meant to be. I am still happening and unfolding. I am still discovering and learning that there are places where I still hide my truth from myself. This is why I will never stop my Mirror Ritual.

"Mirror Ritual is fundamental to our health, immune system and our growth on every level. It is absolutely critical to love yourself." (Heissler, 2017)

Chapter Seven: Power of Words

We live in a society where words are afforded multiple meanings, and some of them are conflicting. We are meant to communicate with others, to speak our truth and share our experiences with these words. When you don't know exactly what you mean, how can you share your message clearly?

This is about you being clear about the message you are conveying. When you communicate with someone via email, text message or over the phone, there is no face to face communication. A large part of communication is nonverbal, so when you take away the opportunity for people to receive those nonverbal cues, you are losing some of the effectiveness of your message. It is much easier to communicate back and forth in person so both parties can clarify and ask questions so they understand. You back up your power with presence.

You are the one that gives the words you speak and hear power. You interpret the meaning of words you hear from others and you decide the meaning of the words you share with others.

Your words reflect what you know about yourself. For this reason, the Power of Words is about understanding how you define words, and the deeper understanding of self. How you understand is directly linked to your life experiences. You have learned untruths about what some words mean. This practice helps you understand and reprogram the old meanings with your truth.

Look at the word **selfish** for example.

Write down your first thoughts about how you define the word selfish. Is your definition of selfish about the word or the trait of a person? If it is more about an unfavorable trait in a person, then your definition of selfish is a judgment. This reflects your experience of the word.

The word selfish can also trigger strong emotions or an unwillingness to look at it. Trigger words will be addressed later on in the chapter. If selfish triggers strong emotions, try replacing it with **self-full**. The true meaning after all, is someone who takes care of themselves first.

To Begin

You will require a book of blank paper and a pencil to begin this practice. The first few pages will be set aside for listing the words you have defined inside. On the first two pages, write "definitions" at the top. On the third page write "trigger words" at the top. List your words in columns in the order they are received. They are not to be organized alphabetically or categorized in any way. Over time you will be able to look back at your list of words and there may be a pattern to observe. When you can see the patterns you will also come to understand something deeper about you.

Your words may come to you on your own. It is recommended that you seek Guidance on this topic.[7]

Some words have very simple meanings, and some are far more complex. You must never seek your definitions from a dictionary. The purpose here is to create your own based on your unique wisdom and experience. A dictionary holds an unemotional and detached definition and will not help your progress.

Writing about it all helps. It is always recommended to write with a wood pencil, as it is a much closer connection to the Earth than a mechanical pencil or plastic pen with ink.

Trigger Words

Because your definitions are created by your thoughts and experiences, some words will bring up old wounds. Trigger words belong in a special list because they take you away from yourself. They may irritate you until you explode or shut down. These words require special care and Guidance.[7] Working with trigger words helps you to take back the power of the trigger. When a trigger word holds no more power over you, you have won a battle and your true definition can shine through.

[7] Guidance is a service that Jessica offers through Budding Hearts Academy and is available for purchase in one or five hour blocks. See www.buddingheartsacademy.com for more information and to book your Guidance appointment or package.

Remember that words are words. You supply the meaning. The practice of understanding words is the practice of understanding self. You are reflected in everything you do, create, everyone you meet, and the way you see and hear.

Words to Eliminate

There are some words that you can eliminate from your repertoire now. Words that have never and will never serve you. The following are a list of these words.

Just

This word minimizes what you are speaking about, making it smaller. No one is ever "just" anything. Just, has no business being used before any living thing, action, outcome or feeling. Using just is an attempt to make what comes after it smaller or insignificant. If you do this to yourself, correct yourself by leaving it out. If you find someone else defining what you do as just this or just that, you may be projecting yourself as less than and that is exactly how they understand you.

Can't

This is the word of someone who does not believe they can. It is a word of someone who is refusing to take responsibility, and in effect, a victim of circumstance.

Replace with Won't

This is the word you use instead of can't. This word leads to choice. For example:

"I can't do my math" versus "I won't do my math". You absolutely can do your math, and for whatever reason you don't want to. Sit with each can't you notice and shift it to won't. This will allow you the opportunity to investigate why you have made yourself a victim of circumstance.

Problem

This is a trigger word for the vast majority of people. It implies that we need a solution, and that we are unable to move forward without one.

Replace with Situation

This is the word you use in place of problem. This is all it ever is...a situation that you find yourself in. Situations shift and change effortlessly, often without you ever being aware. This is a much more neutral thought and does not in any way create a block for the action that may be required.

For example: "I have a problem" versus "I have a situation".

Just saying the first statement out loud, you may feel heavier than you need to. Similar to a math problem in school, if you are not sure of how to begin the process of solving it, you may feel like you are blocked. On the contrary, if you say aloud "I have a situation," it doesn't feel so heavy. You have learned that a problem has a solution. It is unnecessary to "solve" a situation because it doesn't need it. Consider how the situation could change so forward movement could be made instead. Maybe it needs to sit and figure itself out. The difference is subtle yet profound.

Don't, not, no

These are words that allow you to continually focus on the opposite of what you want.

Eliminate these words by asking yourself, when you have noticed yourself using them, "what DO I want?" Take a moment to consider what you do want and then speak that truth. By speaking about what you don't want, you are attracting those things you don't want to you. This is the very basic law of attraction.

If you would like more support on this topic, get a hold of Michael Lozier's book *The Law of Attraction: The Science of Attracting More of What You Do Want and Less of What You Don't*. It is for sale on Amazon.

Perfect

This can be a dangerous word, and also a trigger word for many. It is used flippantly in the media and by people everywhere. Society has an unhealthy infatuation with perfection. Many people seem to be striving for it, when it is simply unachievable. Even the Guides on the Other Side admit to not being perfect. Why not strive to be you? There is no such thing as perfect, and besides, imperfection is much easier to achieve. In fact, you are already there! So, why not accept yourself, your situations and the people in your life the way they already are?

This word also has a lot to do with expectations. Beware when you use this word that you are not creating an expectation of a situation happening exactly as you wish it would, or someone acting exactly how you want them to. When you create expectations, it is highly unlikely that you are sharing with everyone around you exactly what things need to look like, be like, feel like, etc. Even if you have written out a clearly defined list of expectations, there is always room for interpretation.

Should

This is a word that is also linked to expectations. When you use this word, you identify that there is an expectation for you to do something. This is a word used by people who overload themselves with the ideas of things they feel they "should" do. It is actually a form of complaining.

In an earlier chapter you read that complaining about something never helps. Step up to the plate and change it, or in this case, change your words. Do you really want to do this thing you are saying you "should" do? If your answer is yes, do it. If your answer is no, stop.

Try

Do or do not, there is no try. You are either in the process of doing or you are not doing it. As with "should", if you do not want to do something, simply be honest. The world will not fall apart because you say no. There is always a way to get something done. For example: You have a guest arriving and you know they have food allergies, so you go to the store, read labels and spend a lot of time and effort picking out what you have decided is something they can eat. When they arrive, you show them what you got just for them, only to learn that they cannot eat it. Where many people go here, is "well, I tried."

There is no try, there is only do or do not. For this example the best place to determine what a person with food allergies can eat is that person. Ask them. That is doing. If you are uncertain about what to get, because it is a huge undertaking, a discussion with the person may be all you need. Although it feels wonderful to be inclusive, when you don't do your due diligence, you are often left feeling poorly and not being inclusive.

Chapter Eight: The Personal Mantra

As the physical and spiritual are supported with Mirror Ritual, the verbal and auditory are supported through your Personal Mantra.

When your personal mantra is spoken, you are hearing it inside your head and outside your head. Something happens when you hear yourself speak powerful words. You connect with it and may even feel it. When you say your mantra enough, you will become it. After all, you will say it like you mean it every morning and every night as the very last part of your Mirror Ritual once you have discovered you love yourself. It is your spoken commitment to YOU.

Just as Mirror Ritual is for integrating acceptance and love into your subconscious mind, your Personal Mantra is for integrating your commitment to yourself into your life.

For Example:

"Today, I love myself totally and I allow myself the moments I need to nourish my Self as One."

The Personal Mantra is your promise. Your promise might change over time as you align with who you really are. This process and what your personal mantra develops into will be just as unique as you are. It needs to be a completely honest statement and reminder of who you are and how you support yourself to be this person.

My Experience

After using my mantra for a couple years, I said it one day and realized that I was not integrating it into my life. To me this meant I was not being totally honest with myself. While allowing myself the moments I needed to nourish me was a wonderful intention and in line with my journey, I wasn't sure that I was actually living up to my promise.

When I considered my mantra and dissected it, I came up with a few questions that I needed to ask myself to bring my actions into alignment. I needed this to serve as my check in each evening to determine that I was living in line with what I was promising. My Personal Mantra is the reminder of my intention every morning.

I celebrate what I did do, rather than feel sorry or ashamed for what I didn't. I remember that I always begin again tomorrow.

What matters most is that your Personal Mantra is honest and clear. To be an honest and clear statement, take the time to ensure you are integrating it into your day to day. When your intention is clear, your road appears.

My Personal Mantra

Use the space on the next two pages to begin to identify your promise to you. When it is complete, take a photo and email it to buddingheartsacademy@gmail.com for feedback.

Your Personal Mantra....continued

Chapter Nine: The Postulate

Speaking your truth with a clear understanding of words allows you the opportunity to observe miracles.

In the last chapter, while discussing the don't, not and no; you read about the vibration you radiate when you identify what you don't want, versus the vibration you send out when you talk about what you do want. Making a choice about your vibration is how YOU CREATE your REALITY.

You are responsible for your environment, the people around you, and everything you are doing and saying. Looking at life this way is a positive and powerful choice. It puts you in the driver's seat of your experience.

Your present moment is not forever, it is fleeting. When you focus on the lack of what you have, you are projecting that your present moment extends into your future. Not having what you want right now is actually a powerful tool! Your awareness that your situation is not ideal is the first step in projecting what you WANT into the future. You can choose to begin walking in any direction at any moment, in any area of your life.

To create your new experience your intention needs to be clear about your vision. Who do you want to be? Where do you see yourself? How do you see yourself? What is your ideal environment like? What do you want to be doing? What do you feel happy doing?

There are many questions to consider. In chapter five, you discovered Transcendental Elemental Meditation, or TEM™, which you may already be practicing. Ask these questions in your TEM™ practice and see what you notice.

Take full responsibility for your own transformation. Sit with the following two questions on pages 91 and 92 in meditation (see chapter five) and notice the wisdom that comes to you. It may take a few times for the wisdom to flow. Once it comes, put your wisdom in the space provided.

To manifest what you really want, you need to be clean and clear in your thoughts and behaviors and able to step into the flow of the energy at the center of your being. When you begin to apply the Foundation of Fire to your life, you are already stepping into your power. Your ability to manifest exists in how you FEEL about what you want.

Manifesting is about YOU creating or attracting what you want through time and space. The Postulate is about releasing what you want to the energy of the universe and trusting that what you want will come. The two are fundamentally different. Your Postulate is not something you check on after you release it. That would be like decluttering your closet and putting the discarded items in another closet. Trust in the process is important. When you trust that something will come through for you, you can forget about it altogether.

Who am I?

What do I really want?

The Ritual

There are a few simple steps involved in this Ritual.[8]

Step One

Identify what you want. This is why you wrote out what you wanted on the previous page. Your first step is already done! This will change for you as time goes on. You can be as specific or as general as you wish. Be mindful of your words. It is helpful to have someone take a look at what you want for clarity.

Step Two

Take three Activation Breaths and tune into your own energy center. Imagine the full sensory experience of what you want being your reality (sights, sounds, feels, tastes, etc.). This is similar to daydreaming about what you want. Put yourself into the experience and keep on breathing.

Step Three

As you continue to breathe into the experience of having everything you want, create a Purple Bubble around it with your breath.

[8] Having performed postulates on my own and in group settings, I have developed a way for you to sit with yourself and complete it on your own with a FREE download at the Budding Hearts Academy website. It is also part of your BONUSES, so please visit www.foundationoffire.com and select "Download my BONUSES".

Step Four

With your experience of what you want inside your Purple Bubble, offer it up to your Guides. As they accept your dream from you, repeat the following:

Please bring this dream to me.

Step Five

Continue to breathe until the bubble disappears from your sight. Take three final Activation Breaths and with each exhalation say aloud as energetically as you can:

I release this!

Step Six

Finally, remove the page you wrote down what you want on, take it outside in a metal bowl and light it on fire. Once there are only ashes left, toss the contents of the bowl into the air and allow the wind to carry away any last physical remnants of your asking, while stating again three times:

I release this!

Once you are complete, take some time to do something that you enjoy. When you find your mind coming back what you want, the following phrase can be repeated aloud while using your "magic hand" to swipe from right to left in front of your eyes:

I trust the universe provides for me.

It is in this releasing of your vision that you are allowing the energy of the universe to work for you. A watched pot never boils. Think gratitude rather than impatience whenever you can.

Expression

There is this beautiful song called *Fly,* about a woman who is letting go of the past and understanding the power that existed within her all along. The chorus goes like this:

I don't want to live someone else's life.
I am so tired of my silent cry.
It's time to spread my wings and fly. (Fly, 2016)

Expression is the only way you can share your giftedness. It doesn't have to be public video blogs, or writing a book, or recording music. It can be simple. It might be doing your best at the vocation you have chosen. It might be listening to people and providing support. It might be providing an example to your children about how to live in balance. It might be creating in the arts, or providing psychic readings or simply being you. It might be giving your energy at a job to support your family.

It is how you are your authentic self. How do you express yourself?

Use the table on the following pages to identify what you do for personal expression and how often. Remember to be honest, and place one form of expression in each row. The point is not to fill as many boxes as you can. It is for you to identify how you express yourself and if you are doing it as much as you need to. When you aren't expressing yourself freely, you are depressing yourself. If you don't typically express yourself, you may need to discover your motivation.

How I Express Myself	How Often?

How I express myself	How often?

Chapter Ten: Motivation

Motivation is the force that encourages you to express yourself and your gifts. Most people have some form of motivation, or reason, that they do what they do.

My Experience

My motivators have changed over the years. When I was considering where to go for my post-secondary education, my motivation was to go to the school with the shortest medical program that also offered undergraduate degrees. I didn't want to change cities or school after creating connections.

Just before I left for post-secondary school, I was diagnosed with late stage degenerative bone disease. At nineteen years old I had the bone structure of a sixty-five year old! While the diagnosis I received explained the near constant pain I was in, why I was unable to stand for long periods of time and a host of other situations I was experiencing, I had difficulty accepting the prognosis I was given. I was told that given the advanced age of my bones, by the time I was thirty-five years old I would be unable to support my body and be confined to a wheel-chair, most likely addicted to pain medications in an effort to stop the pain. What rose up inside me as a teenager on the cusp of adulthood was powerful. While I indulged in the pity party that came with sharing the diagnosis and prognosis I received, I never stopped moving.

The morning after the first round of try outs for my university basketball team four months later, which consisted of running a six minute mile then showing off my insane basketball skills in the gym for two hours; I was unable to physically roll over in bed. I was unable to soldier through the excruciating pain I was experiencing, or move, so I called to cancel my place in the second round of try outs that morning. I was devastated. I was told back surgeries were all that could be done for the condition I had.

For the next two years I had no motivation, I simply went through the motions of getting up, eating, going to work, going to school and surviving. Then one day I met a guy. He was super cute, the attraction was bonkers strong and something changed. The next morning, I woke up early, showered and did my hair, applied the bit of makeup and wowed him. He motivated me to care about how I looked. For the rest of my time in school, he was my motivation to pull up my grades. He seemed to breathe life back into me. He was the first person that I ever felt empowered me, though I am certain many tried.

He helped me believe that I wasn't the diagnosis I was given. I felt the first glimmer of possibility that I could strengthen my body. We loved camping together, and I wanted to be able to go anywhere with him. I went to a chiropractor and began focused rehabilitative exercises to reclaim mobility, flexibility and achieve natural pain relief.

After the first year I could do my commute to work without pain. That was huge! My motivation grew and I listened to my intuition. I learned about how refined foods and sugars created inflammation and how there was a possible link to my condition, so I began making changes to my diet and of course this wonder of a man did it right along with me.

Over the next few years I continued my healing journey, getting deeper into food choices and began making everything from scratch. I learned I was intolerant to grains and my boyfriend was allergic to conventional dairy products. I began making all our food from scratch and eliminated dairy. My health was improving every day. By the time I was 26 I could ride a bike without my hips seizing and I could do nearly any activity without debilitating pain. I refused to take pain modifiers, even for a headache and rested when I needed to. I learned that when I am motivated I can achieve anything!

After we were married we wanted to start a family. We tried for 6 months with no success. I felt a knowing inside that I was unable to conceive. This motivated me to see a naturopath. I charted every little thing about my body I could, and one of the 10 things I was charting and graphing daily was my basal body temperature. My erratic temperature revealed I was iodine deficient. This may not seem like a big deal, but iodine is food for the thyroid gland, which controls body temperature. Without it, my body couldn't maintain a constant body temperature and without that my body would never successfully host a pregnancy.

My naturopath directed me to synthetic iodine and thirteen days later, I was pregnant! I was always reinforcing that my intuition was correct. I listened, followed it and did what was necessary to achieve what I wanted.

I turned 35 years old on April 13th, 2017. Today I am pain free, have competed in two Tough Mudders, go interior camping yearly, run a successful spiritual development business, and have three beautiful children. The diagnosis I received when I was nineteen is no longer relevant. My bones are thirty-five years old. My life is better than my wildest dreams!

I recognize my spiritual development was smoother because I live a lifestyle that is in alignment with who I really am. This motivated me to write my first book in 2010 and revamp it for 2017. Be on the look out for Lifestyle Change Made Easy, expected to release in the summer of 2017.

Now, my motivation to move forward is my children. When I am true to myself, I am an example to my children that they can be too. They are three incredibly gifted children and I know they will be game changers for the future. I step into myself every morning in my mirror and stay true to my heart for them.

Your motivation can come from absolutely anywhere. Don't judge where your motivation comes from. As long as you are being true to who you are, it is all good.

What motivates you?

The Becoming Journey

I lay on the table at The Gathering Place, ready for my first energy session in about 6 months.

Once I smelled the smoke of sage and breathed deeply, I was at the flat rock where Grandfather met me in the beginning. I was standing there at the mouth of the cave. I did not notice whether there was a fire burning or not. He did not wait for me to say anything, and he didn't hug me. Instead he said, "I have been waiting for you." Of course he had. He is always waiting for me.

When I am in his presence I am always filled with an indescribable feeling of being at home. It is pure acceptance and love. Today there was a tinge of impatience. Grandfather moved into the cave and invited me to come with him. This was new. I had never been inside the cave before. I thanked him for allowing me into his cave. He looked at me and smiled his knowing smiled and told me that this has always been my cave.

My cave! In all the years that I have been guiding people to journey into their own sacred spaces, I realized in this moment that I had yet to journey into my own. I had flown on the back of Grandfather's back when he was a Raven. He has taken me to my past and we have discussed my gifts, my name and so much more. Never in a million years did I ever see this coming.

I looked around with the realization that this was my cave settling in. What I noticed and was drawn to was a huge rock slide around the outer edge of the cave. I walked over to take a look and Grandfather handed me the Bear skin cloak that had always gone around my shoulders. This time it was folded up and he said, "for beneath you, for your ride." I was a little unsure and asked him if that would dishonor my mother, to sit on her skin and ride her down a slide. He only chuckled and told me that if I didn't use it I would hurt my backside on the rocks. He also told me I would need it for later. I know better than to ask questions. I put the skin at the top of the slide, sat down and pushed myself forward.

Round and round and down and down I went. It happened fast. The sensation I was feeling was one I had been fighting for years. It had been happening to me when I least expected it and I would need my husband to help me get to our bed so I could sleep it off. It was always uncomfortable until this moment. I was headed further within to a place I would not previously allow myself to go. At this moment I was ready for it. I laughed out loud and let out a whoop as I slid down this spiral rock slide to the bottom.

When I came to a stop I was in a large open cavern. To my left there was a pool of water and I knew it was the Sacred First Waters of Femininity. To my right was another pool of water and I knew it was the Sacred First Waters of Masculinity....the becoming water. I did not remember ever learning this or hearing about them. I simply had an inner knowing.

I walked over to the Sacred Feminine Water and put my arm in up to my shoulder then pulled it back out. My physical body back on the massage table at The Gathering Place was tingling all over. I had a flash back of a conversation with Two Claws the night previous when he told me that dipping our toes in was never enough. I had said, "We need to jump right in." So I did. I jumped into the Sacred Water. My whole body was tingling. I immediately shape shifted into Otter and played around for a moment. When I came back to the edge of the rock, I saw that The Thirteen Grandmothers were waiting for me, each watching me with a smile on their faces, each so wonderfully beautiful and magical.

When I climbed out of the water I was myself again, naked and wet and tingling all over. Ohm Ma, Grandmother of the Void, came and guided me to a rock that was sitting between the two waters. I sat down on the Bear skin cloak that was draped over the rock. The Grandmothers each took turns painting wings on my back. The wings covered my entire back and the patterning was incredible. When the last one had put the last markings on, they turned me toward them. They were all standing in a circle with Eniska, Grandmother of the Womb, standing in the center. She came to me and sat down inside my body. We became one. The Bear skin was wrapped around my body, creating a cocoon, and it was then wrapped again with other things that I have no business knowing about.

I was in total darkness now. I felt warm, cozy, and tingly and a new feeling I couldn't quite put my finger on. When they were done wrapping me up, I was lifted and gently placed on the Sacred Masculine pool of water. I floated for a few moments, and then began to twitch and jump. My body was transforming. On the table at The Gathering Place my body was like a "fish out of water" as Two Claws explained it.

All at once, my coverings began to dissolve from my body, and I sank down into the water. I immediately shape shifted into Salmon and swam as far down as I could, and then turned toward the surface. I knew I had to swim as hard and fast as I could. I did. When I breached the Sacred Water, I turned into a Circopia Moth. My wings held the patterns that were painted on my back by the Grandmothers and I felt a freedom like one I have never known in this lifetime. This freedom was familiar though. I turned toward the Grandmothers and thanked them then flew up and out of the cave. I passed Grandfather sitting at his fire on the rock ledge. He looked up at me smiling the broadest smile I can remember on his face in all my lifetimes combined.

I flew out over the virgin pine forest and up toward the Sun. I flew down near the River and listened to the Water and smelled the scent of life in the forest. I finally came to land on a bunch of little white flowers at the riverside. I took in my surroundings. A white tailed Doe to my right, drinking from the stream. A Red Tailed Hawk was perched in the tree above me.

The Deer left the water's edge and a Great White Wolf came up to have a drink. I could see Salmon and Otter in the River. I could feel the Wind on my wings. Smell the Earth around me, and the Sun was warming me. I am One. I am Home. I am Whole.

When I returned from my journey, Two Claws had tears running down his face. He told me he wasn't sure that I would ever find who I was in this time. He called me Little Flower. This is my name from forever before, when I first walked the Earth with my small tribe of family. When Two Claws was my mate and Grandfather was my Father, I used to put little white flowers between my toes and only smile when the others would ask why. Always knowing and never telling my secret. I still remember why, and I am still never telling. Some truths are better understood by our own hearts.

We are all One,
Jessica Little Flower Smalls

Notes

Notes

Notes

Notes

Works Cited

Dyer, D. W. (2008). *Your Ultimate Calling: 365 Ways to Bring Inspiration into Your Life.* China: Hay House Inc.

Heissler, M. (2016, October). (J. Smalls, Interviewer)

Heissler, M. (2017, March). (J. Smalls, Interviewer)

Marshall III, J. M. (2001). *The Lakota Way: stories and lessons for living - native american wisdom on ethics and character.* New York: Penguin Compass.

Smalls, J. (Performer). (2016). Fly. Petrolia, Ontario, Canada.